Looking for Poems
on the Swamp Rabbit Trail

poems by

Susan Stetson Renault

Finishing Line Press
Georgetown, Kentucky

Looking for Poems
on the Swamp Rabbit Trail

ACKNOWLEDGMENTS

Special thanks, computer tutor, Cada McCoy, Poetry friend and master disentangler of colliding Pages and Word docs. She rescued both poet and poems from an unhappy kerfuffle.

*Thanks, Emmie Watson for your kind words!

Publisher: Leah Huete de Maines
Editor: Christen Kincaid
Cover Art: Zander Renault
Author Photo: Marie Eldridge, neighbor
Cover Design: Zander Renault

Order online: www.finishinglinepress.com
also available on amazon.com

Author inquiries and mail orders:
Finishing Line Press
PO Box 1626
Georgetown, Kentucky 40324
USA

Contents

"Instructions for living a life.
Pay attention.
Be astonished.
Tell about it."
—Mary Oliver

The day I watched a heron take flight

This morning waited for me all my life,
the perfect sun above
silent heron-of-the-lakeside
the moment
heaven pleased
he must
aloft and glide.
This morning knew, when I was born,
a lake at rest midst winter trees
whispering its peace
the very moment
heaven'd pleased;
it waited for me
all my life.

The day I faced a choice

What if I chose today
to organize my closet
perfectly;
summer, fall, winter, spring
darks together
lighter ones beside
instead of taking Bluebelle
for a ride,
instead of cycling
threw away old socks
while Monarchs waited
in the sun?

The day I watched Slow Dog (1)

I watch Slow Dog
teeter on tired legs,
collapse onto lame hips,
settle softly upon his grassy spot
at the side of the trail,
a favorite resting spot.
The Man holds the slack leash
in his crooked hand
and waits. He can see his house
ten minutes, at most,
(once, a two-minute sprint),
Slow Dog doesn't move. "You know,"
I whisper; "he cannot hear,
your man with the cloudy eyes
and the crooked hands
and the voice so soft it has almost disappeared."

The day I watched Slow Dog (2)

"Go on, now. Get him home
Let him hang up his leash
Tomorrow you will sit by the sunny window, and
the next day and the day after that
on the fleecy couch
with two worn cushions shaped
by two old friends
who once sprinted
like the wind
leash taut
two minutes
like greyhounds."

The day we followed a voice that took us to Joseph

How would I have known if she hadn't wiggled me away
from my desk and turned me urgently to Bluebelle leaning
next to the door and prodded us two directly to the bike
trail? How would I have known if the voice hadn't insisted,
"Look up, look up, and pushed my shoulders back and lifted
my chin to see him watching us, hawk proud in his mottled
orange vest and cinnamon-streaked cap…his silver back,
crisscrossed and checkered sun and ashes, his yellow beak,
brown leggings as if flaked with snow, and tawny shoulders?
How would we have known he would make us stop and we
would look up and we would name him Joseph?

The day I cycled over Woodland Hill. Go Girl!

When I was seventy-six, I pedaled my bicycle
over Woodland Hill and arrived on the other side
at age twenty, full of myself. I thought
of turning around and pedaling
back up and over the hill to where I'd begun,
but where I'd begun wasn't there anymore,
the daunting ascent no longer there,
even the voices who said I couldn't do it,
even the voices were gone.

The day I discovered how hawks flirt

One sweep of the sky
would do, silent as a cloud
soft as sunlight. One
magnificent sweep of the air
above her tree, but he does two.

She knows his grace too grand
for sky alone, she knows
proud upon her branch
silent as a shadow
her grace too grand
for branch alone.
She does not move.
He knows.

The day I became a puddle-riding girl (1)

Today I will ride through puddles
and know no harm from
wet ankles, just joy. I will scale a hill
I've never climbed before
and know I can scale
the next one too.
I will name the sticks
strewn across my path
from morning storms:
chewed-cigar stick,
the squid,
almost-thought-you-were-a turtle stick.
I will stop for red coneflowers
near lavender stalks
because their red urgency
is meant to be obeyed.
I will imitate
the creaking sound
from a thick wet tree,
of a bird/frog/toad/ or jungle
something I cannot see, an
ungreased door on a crooked cellar floor
warped and tight,
creeach, again, I will recite
twenty times until I get it right.

The day I became a puddle-riding girl (2)

When the rain begins
and I must choose
forward or turn back
which way to go,
I will know:
a puddle-riding girl who scales new hills, names
the sticks, learns to creeach,
she knows.

The day we called a perfect summer day

They're fighting over me again today:
ferocious sun to lay her chunky fingers
upon my path,
knuckled and random:
delicious, shadowy
weaver, cathedral maker, braided thick
by summer's wet love;
all I have to do
is show up.

The day I watch a tiny chipmunk skitter up hill

I cycle the Swamp Rabbit Trail
so I will recall on sleepless nights
the dry hiss of crisp leaves
whispering
along my path

so I will recall one leaf
turning autumn red
alone among her sisters
who will soon
follow her boldness

so I will recall the tiny chipmunk
who summits the trail's shoulders
and never stops
to worry
they are too high.

The day I spread extra verses to the wind

If you walk or bike this trail
looking for a poem and fail
to find your muse, feel free to use
a verse or two I knew
briefly, until they grew
too big to keep
inside my head,
and so I spread them on the wind,
on spring puddles and within
small cracks and burrows,
brittle wings of tiny things
that hover over summer mud,
some landing like a mite of dust
and others with a thud.
Take the extra word I cast:
quick, lithe, stormy, sinister
and vast
and all the tunes my heart released
for your own poem, poems and peace.
commit them to your heart, then, please,
whatever you can't use, release.

The day Grandmother Wind filled my mouth with laughter

Grandmother Wind clasps my cheeks in her weathered hands;
my mouth fills with laughter;
sometimes she is gentle as a kiss
sometimes she is full of piss and vinegar

Today I will buffet you, she says.
Buffet? I ask.
yes, she says. If you keep going
in the face of my buffeting, you win.

I will give you a prize, she says.
Look into the winter woods
where bony branches stretch and sun rays reach the ground.
Look, and choose a prize,
anything you want:

a dream, a wish, a scratchy sound
a poem, a song, a glimpse of squirrel
whose cheeks bulge
with stuffing for his winter rest,

joy to place upon your pillow
beside your head when you seek sleep,
what will you choose?

I will choose to keep going, I say
what if your legs become weary,
whining because they do not
take their labors lightly? she asks.

I will tell them, Hush, I say,
listen to the poetry I found in the woods
listen to Grandmother Wind who clasps my cheeks in her hands,
buffets me and fills my mouth with laughter.

The day I knew poets see more than racers do (1)

The spandex guys fly
muscled legs spinning
spinning. In their eyes pity
for this old girl pumping,
panting, who will never know
the thrill of victory flashing
passing all the others on the trail.
I'm much too slow,
I'll never win and always fail.
My eyes catch butterflies;
I talk to birds, swoon at breezes,
stop for squirrels
when it pleases,
and will never know the thrill
of speeding up the hill.

The day I knew poets see more than racers do (2)

It's true, the racers
soaring free may
win the prize and pity me,
but their poor eyes
that do not see
the herons, turtles and the
deer are to be pitied and
their ears, deaf to a thousand
raucous chirps and tweets,
alas, will never know
the symphonies
that fill these paths.
A racer, spinning, winning,
driven, never wonders
if the whisper
a morning breeze was
given just for him, alone,
to surprise his heart
with music
and a poem.

The day I felt very silly

Does a turtle ever wobble
and topple off his log
into a bog, then struggle to roll upright
as he should?

Does a squirrel ever
stub his toe on wood?
Does a cardinal (mate for life)
ever tweet at the wrong wife
and get in trouble?

Can an owl get high on grub
and miss his branch at night
because he's seeing double?

Has a rattler ever coiled himself
completely in a knot? Or a mockingbird
stop short because she just forgot
the words (a senior moment rare in birds)?

Could a goose lose his place in classic V formation,
heading South instead of North,
leaving total consternation?

Could a deer miss his mark and bump into a tree,
spin around, seeing stars,
buckling to his knees?

What if someone oldish grew younger every time
she rode her bike?
What would that be like?

The day a white-tailed deer took my breath away

I share, cannot bear
the dizzying fulness alone
how I cycled the hill with my head bent low
and lifted my eyes as the white tail
melted into the bushes
silent as dew.

If I go to bed with this radiance,
I will not sleep.
If I wake and leave it
upon my pillow,
my feet will not dance
as they should.

Joy, unshared, is gluttony, a table awaiting
dinner for one.

The day I pretended to be a child in the Children's Garden

There are no children here today
so I will stand curious as a cat,
my two hands clasped behind
my back and recite
the garden alphabet: H, I, J
hollyhock, iris, Joe Pye Weed—

I sing Joe Pye, Joe Pye,
stuck a finger in his eye
sweet blushing Irish miss
made him better
with a kiss.

 I will promise not to pull or pluck a single stalk
but leave these blossom friends
for real children and watch
with this day's curiosity
for what a child might do alone
in a Children's Garden:
touch a petal softly
with one finger
and put her nose close
to know its spicy fragrance
nestle in the crook of the Chaste tree,
reaching for the sky, Old Joe Pye
couldn't whistle if he tried,
wait for someone to come alongside
my pretty nest and see how perfectly
I rest in leafy arms like
a mother's hug
tree love.

The day a catalpa tree reminded me of Christine

Isn't it wonderful when you see something, and
it reminds you of something else:
winter mittens, mom's knitting;
a puppet show, a London holiday;
a ride to Ipswich, the Clam Box.

Today I cycle homeward
along the Swamp Rabbit Trail,
outstretched branches dangling
slender pods above, and just like that
we are together,
14 Rowland Street,
under your catalpa;

we pull our wicker chairs onto the lawn;
under her shady arms. Our children run around
her ample trunk. The leaves are shaped
like hearts and
you serve me ginger tea:

ginger tea, my friend Christine.

The day I laughed at the raucous Bird Singers

Freedom Singers,
from the treetops
F-R-E-E-D-O-M
from wrong notes
dissenting opinions,
haughty eyes
of prettier birds,
tweet your lover, trill duets
live abundantly
F-R-E-E-D-O-M
from embarrassment
imperfection, BIG HIPS,
You are BIRD
YOU SING!

Claim your branches,
scatter a thousand new notes
to the clouds,
wake every sleeping thing
let freedom ring
not too old nor young
not unseasoned nor overripe
NO APOLOGIES
free to be good enough
for outrageous celebration
to address the sun directly,
passionate, fearless
address the sun driectly
Sassy free bird.

The day I wanted to leap into a hammock

Across the wide-empty field,
like a smile beckoning an old friend,
a hammock stretches quiet between two oaks.

If I wanted I could lay my tired bike
beside the trail, sprint across the-empty-field,
swing tanned legs into the waiting web

like riding a bike, I'd say,
like a gymnast
or a cat
you never forget

I could stretch like a memory, twist
fingers around the hammock's ropy weave,
leave miles and years behind,

still breathless from pedaling,
I could leap if I wished,
nest like a wee, small bird

in strings and mesh,
feel hammock arms
around me, become a child.
I could if I wanted.

I could lay my tired bike down
and run across the field
climb aboard the hammock, close my eyes.

On another day.

The day I eulogized a dead leaf

Hail, dead sister, dried and sere
won't live to see another year
wrinkled, crisp, wind-tossed. Perchance
you're dreaming of the dance
when breezes swept you light aloft, soft so soft.

Oh, dead sister, don't you know
if you were just a little younger
still ablush with nature's brush
a passerby might pluck you, later to arrange
and tuck you in amongst yellow gourds,
orange berries, golden grasses with their feathery heads
and place you on a mantel to recall for all
the artistry of fall.

Oh, dead sister, do you know
that after fall and after snow
and after life's eternal dream, once more
your frosty tears unseen
will melt into the fragrant earth,
the dance of life goes on. Let go.
Let go. We'll see you yet again and you,
my lovely wrinkled friend, will be made new.
Let go. Let go.
Let go.

The day I talked to the shadows

Today I will ride my bicycle
to the Swamp Rabbit Trail
and talk to the shadows.
Thank you for your caress
on my damp shoulders
when days are hot, I will say.
Your playful puddles of shade,
tea cups and saucers and wobbly
widows wattles drape heavily
along my path and make me laugh,
large and small and playful,
what shall I give you in return?
"Sing," they tell me,
"Like you did on our first day."

The day I read Darrell's trail bench

Did the river banks learn
the rhythm of his feet upon the trail?
Did the flowers inhale
the soapy scent from a morning shower?
Did they know the thrilling power
of a young man's stride
and dreams
lanky legs
kicking high
chasing the wind?
Did cherry blossoms know
when the air became still
and weep
did they wait?
and wait?

And, I, who pedal past murky swamp,
brambles where sparrows peck,
redbuds scrunched upon their limbs,
squirrels with praying hands,
robins listening for worms…
Am I the breath
upon their leaves?
When I go
will they know
there is a space
where once
a poem was born?
Will they wait?
And mourn?

The day I wanted to be the music for someone who is tired

Blessed is the one who
travels under leafy shade
and gives her peaceful coolness
to another who is parched.

Blessed is the one who hears a bird
and her smile is like a song for
another who is tired.

Blessed is she whose heart has
fluttered on butterfly wings
and gives her story to
another who has forgotten
how to dance.

The day I observed a solitary heron

If the Lord should come to call,
I'd like him
to appear in Fall, and if
I might be extra bold,
on a sunny morning that is
cold enough to send a chill

beneath my cuffs
(but not so frosty that
my breath comes out in puffs).

Perhaps—I'm really pushing here—
a solitary heron, standing near,
up to his knees in water
will catch my eye.

Together we will know
our time has come to fly.

The day I named a flower Estelle

If I were a namer of things, I would
happily greet the roses, lace, and honeysuckle,
but never would allow a flower of mine
be called *ragwort*, or much worse, *mare's fart*,
stinky nanny. Any namer of things can only cringe
at the foul fermented image of a dark gray cloth
wiping grandpa's phlegmy cough.

I would
instead find un bon mot to tell how golden
each fine petal dances daisy-like atop a slender stem,
bursts like tiny fireworks and winks
at me small stars splashed with sunlight,
I would call her name Estelle
and she would forever dwell
along my favorite paths
if I were a namer of things.

Sue grew up with two harbors and an ocean surrounding her small New England town. She learned to swim, find clams, and climb the rocks at a young age. She was a collector: sea shells, beach glass and smooth stones. These became jewelry and window sill sun-collectors. She believed nothing could pull her from her New England roots.

Years later, though, all grown up, she & Lance followed a job change to Greenville, South Carolina; years after that they retired and became downtown city dwellers… with Greenville's brand new Swamp Rabbit Trail biking/walking path meandering past their "back yard." When Sue had a series of hip surgeries, she turned to the trail for exercise and recovery, healing one mile at a time. The trail was kind to her, filling her spirit with playful squirrels, squawky cardinals and the fellow she called her heron friend. In no time at all, she was collecting again and discovering all over the fun of tucking something new into her basket. She collected the sounds of the trees. She collected stories of the other trail runners and riders. She collected poetry flowers and heart-shaped leaves. Now, she takes these home and turns them into her own heart's joy. She writes their poetry and gives it to you.

www.ingramcontent.com/pod-product-compliance
Lightning Source LLC
Chambersburg PA
CBHW022056080426
42734CB00009B/1372